An American Composer Charles E. Ives: New England Transcendentalism

Dr. Paul A. Rodríguez

Copyright © 2016
Cogito Consulting, LLC
Dr. Paul A. Rodriguez
All rights reserved.
ISBN-10: 0-9863965-3-3
ISBN-13: 978-0-9863065-3-2

DEDICATION

For my children, Paul, Alex and Harmonie. I dedicate this manuscript so that they may gain knowledge and interest in philosophy and music.

CONTENTS

	Dedication	iii
	Acknowledgments	vii
1	Chapter Introduction	1
2	Chapter Influence of Ralph Waldo Emerson on Charles E. Ives's Aesthetic	13
3	Chapter Henry David Thoreau's Contributions to Ives's Aesthetics Development	45
4	Chapter Conclusion	81
	References	93
	Discography	112
	About Author	113

ACKNOWLEDGMENTS

I wish to acknowledge Dr. Nors S. Josephson for his unceasing patience and consistent encouragement throughout this endeavor. I thank my parents for their support, Salvador Z. Rodríguez (RIP 1992), especially my mother, Maria Fernandez Rodríguez (RIP 1991), for her sacrifices and time spent typing this paper.

CHAPTER 1

INTRODUCTION

Much interest has been shown in Charles Ives since his death on May 19, 1954. Few composers in the history of music have offered the innumerable problems of analysis and performance that are seen in the works of Ives. Although the importance of this major American composer is now widely recognized, the frustrating complexity of his music has succeeded in discouraging large-

Dr. Paul A. Rodríguez

scale studies of Ives's compositional characteristics on a musicological level.

Ives's transcendental beliefs directly influenced his concepts of freedom in creative expression. For this reason, this book will focus on Ives's indebtedness to Ralph Waldo Emerson, Henry Thoreau, Horatio Parker ad George Ives.

This book begins with an investigation of the New England Transcendental tradition. The Transcendentalists were critical,

An American Composer Charles E. Ives:
New England Transcendentalism

restless, sensitive and highly sophisticated. They were Utopians who seriously reacted to radical social changes, and advocated progressive opinions. Music was very important to them as an expression of their beliefs, and their musical philosophy greatly influenced the development of Ives's musical thought. The Transcendentalists regarded music as a unique form of communication, a universal truth, capable of penetrating all the barriers of time and space.

Dr. Paul A. Rodríguez

Furthermore, they viewed music as a means of communicating with one's own thoughts. Ives's philosophical beliefs about musical composition will be discussed with reference to Ives's own writings on aesthetics and music, as well as selected works by Ralph Waldo Emerson, Henry David Thoreau and others. In addition, Ives's aesthetic concepts are reflected in the structural organization of the above-mentioned piano compositions.

It is not possible within the

An American Composer Charles E. Ives:
New England Transcendentalism

limited scope of this manuscript to present a detailed account of Ives's life. However, there are some biographical considerations and philosophical beliefs that are valuable to this study insofar as they affected Ives's thoughts about music and composition. In particular, the New England Transcendentalists exerted a direct influence upon his concepts of creative freedom and stylistic development.

    Most books and periodicals have considered the influences of

Dr. Paul A. Rodríguez

the New England Transcendentalists upon Ives. However, the sum of his philosophical and musical thoughts exist in his own <u>Memos</u>, <u>Essay Before a Sonata</u>, and handwritten notes made in his manuscripts.

      Sister Mary Ann Joyce's dissertation, "<u>The Three-Page Sonata</u> of Charles Ives: An Analysis and a Corrected Version," presents The Three-Page Sonata from a structural and formal point of view.[1] The author discusses

An American Composer Charles E. Ives: New England Transcendentalism

Ives's use of polytonality, polymeters, asymmetrical phrase structures, polyrhythms, and ambiguous tonal centers.

Nors S. Josephson's article, "Zur formalen Struktur einiger später Orchesterwerke von Charles Ives (1874-1954),"[2] examines the stylistic

---

[1] Sister Mary Ann Joyce, C.S.J., "The Three-Page Sonata of Charles Ives: An Analysis and a Corrected Version." (Ph.D. Dissertation, Washington University, 1970.)

[2] Nors S. Josephson, "Zur formalen Struktur einiger später Orchesterwerke von Charles Ives (1874-1954)," Die Musikforschung 27 (1974), pp. 64-67.

development in Ives's orchestral works of the period from 1911-16. He describes three distinct phases — the abstract, the realist, and the symbolic. Josephson discusses their relationship to three earlier phases of Ives's activity. Ives's development thus emerges as consistent and gradual.

Dennis Marshall's article in <u>Perspectives in New Music</u>, "Charles Ives Quotations: Manner or Substance?"[3]

[3] Dennis Marshall, "Charles Ives's Quotations: Manner or Substance?", Perspectives of New Music 6 (1968): 45-56.

articulates how Ives consciously used borrowed materials for their musical characteristics and interrelationships from the very beginning of the creative process, and how these borrowed elements formed a part of the real substance of his musical art.

Gordon Cyr's article, "Intervallic Structural Elements in Ives's Fourth Symphony,"[4] presents the Fourth Symphony

---

[4] Gordon Cyr, "Intervallic Structural Elements in Ives's Fourth Symphony," Perspectives of New Music 10 (Fall/Winter 1971): 291-303.

Dr. Paul A. Rodríguez

from an intervallic relationship. The author examines Ives's use of borrowed tunes and the alteration of the basic cell by way of inversion, retrograde, and stretto.

Clayton Henderson's dissertation, "Quotation as a Style Element in the Music of Charles Ives,"[5] considers the structural role of borrowed elements as a more significant key for understanding Ives's music. Ives adopted much of his material with

---

[5] Clayton Henderson, "Quotation as a Style Element in the Music of Charles Ives." (Ph.D. Dissertation, Washington University, 1969).

discernment, using it for its programmatic qualities and as a unifying element from which traditional forms, such as rondo, verse and refrain, ternary structure, and arch designs were evolved most frequently.

At present, there are no reliable stylistic analyses and philosophical investigations of <u>Invention</u>, <u>March in G and D "Here's to Good Old Yale"</u>, <u>Three-Page Sonata</u>, <u>Song Without (Good) Words</u>, <u>The Anti-Abolitionist Riots</u>, <u>Some</u>

Dr. Paul A. Rodríguez

<u>Southpaw Pitching</u>, <u>Varied Air and Variations</u>, <u>Waltz Rondo</u>, <u>Study No. 22</u>, <u>The Celestial Railroad</u>. Therefore, it is necessary to emphasize the salient factors which contribute to Ives's compositional characteristics

CHAPTER 2

INFLUENCE OF RALPH WALDO EMERSON ON CHARLES E. IVES'S AESTHETIC

The disposition of an artist is often revealed by a man's choice of archetypal heroes. Charles Ives's hero was Ralph Waldo Emerson. Emerson's idealistic conclusions about life sank deeply into an American

Dr. Paul A. Rodríguez

subconsciousness that wanted to believe that the world was God's and not the Devil's:

> We are wiser than we know. If we will not interfere with our thought, but will act entirely, or see how the thing stands in God, we know the particular thing, and everything, and every man. For the Maker of all things and all persons stands behind us and casts his dread omniscience through us over things.[6]

Emerson conceived <u>America's destiny as a spiritual</u>

[6] Ralph Waldo Emerson, "The Over-Soul," Essays. (Boston: Houghton, Mifflin & Co., 1883), p. 263.

An American Composer Charles E. Ives:
New England Transcendentalism

quest and insistence on the values of the past. Most importantly, the artist or philosopher must build on what has gone before, but he must come to destiny with his own eyes and take from it only what serves to inspire his own thoughts and feelings. Borrowing from the past was one means of transcending the present.

Emerson profoundly believed in quotation. He borrowed from many men and books. For Emerson, there was no disgrace in borrowing. As the author stated in his essay, <u>Quotation and Originality</u>, he borrowed "proudly and royally, as a king borrows from one of his attendants the coin that bears his own image and superscription."[7]

Emerson's world was revealed through abstraction, with similarities seen <u>everywhere.</u> He was somewhat

---

[7] Rosalie Sandra Perry, "Charles Ives and the American Mind." (Ohio: Kent State University Press, 1974), p. 44.

An American Composer Charles E. Ives:
New England Transcendentalism

doubtful about the certainty of man's knowledge of particulars; he thought that the physical world was a creation of the mind:

> We live in succession, in division, in parts, in particles. Meantime within silence; the universal beauty, to which every part and particle is equally related, the eternal ONE. And this deep power in which we exist and who beatitude is all accessible to us, is not only self-sufficing and perfect in every hour, but the act of seeing and the thing seen, the seer and the spectacle, the subject and the object are one.[8]

Dr. Paul A. Rodríguez

One of his important beliefs was that it is not the thing, but the way the thing is said that matters. All things were metaphors, and facts corresponded to spiritual laws. The character of life was conceived as a growing process of expanding fertility:

The simplicity of nature is not that which may easily be read, but is inexhaustible. The last analysis can no wise be made. We judge of a man's wisdom by

---

[8] Ralph Waldo Emerson, "The Over-Soul," Essays. (Boston: Houghton, Mifflin & Co., 1883), p. 253.

his hope, knowing that the perception of the inexhaustibleness of nature is an immortal youth. The wild fertility of nature is felt in comparing our rigid names and reputations without fluid consciousness.[9]

Organic productivity meant that substance was really process.

Ives, too, saw a fundamental significance in the high moral and spiritual values in regard to social and

---

[9] Ralph Waldo Emerson, "Spiritual Laws," Essays. (Boston: Houghton, Mifflin & Col., 1883). p. 92.

economic progress. He found in these same values the most fundamental elements of artistic expression. Ives believed that the principal significance of music originated in the spiritual qualities which it represented. He suggested that all conditions of inspirations seemed closely connected with some actual experience in nature or in society:

. . . if he is willing to use or learn to use (or at least if he is not afraid of trying to use)

An American Composer Charles E. Ives:
New England Transcendentalism

whatever he can of any and all lessons of the infinite that humanity has received and thrown to man, that nature has exposed and sacrificed, . . . he is growing and approaching nearer to perfect truths – whatever they are and wherever they may be.[10]

Since music is representative of a higher spiritual nature, Ives considered all music, even "pure music," as programmatic. He believed

---

[10] Charles E. Ives, Essays Before a Sonata and Other Writings. (New York: Norton & Co., 1964), p. 92.

Dr. Paul A. Rodríguez

that program music customarily makes its appeal to the listener's emotions and thus is commonly viewed as an expression of the sensuous. In its initial conception, this kind of music does not even require that the listener discern a deeper meaning, nor an element in which the intellect has a part. According to this viewpoint, music is a language of the emotions aroused for their own sake, devoid of a higher spiritual value. On the contrary, Ives conceived program music as a deeper spiritual element which has not been reached:

> They do often arouse something that has not yet passed the borderline between subconsciousness and consciousness—an artist intuition. Here is a program!--conscious or subconscious, what does it matter?[11]

In this way, Ives felt that "pure music" could be "programmatic" by being representative of a higher value:

---

[11] Ibid., p. 7.

Dr. Paul A. Rodríguez

The translation of an artistic intuition into musical sounds approving and reflecting, or endeavoring to approve and reflect, a moral goodness, a high vitality, etc.[12]

However, Ives did not feel that the finer distinctions of the lower human sentiments could be represented in music. For him, music could best express transcendental feelings, which could be exposed without undo

---

[12] Charles E. Ives, Essays Before a Sonata and Other Writings. (New York: Norton & Co., 1964), p. 7.

sensitiveness on the part of the composer. Ives viewed music as a transcendent language, which was capable of exposing a wider expression range of philosophical aspirations, rather than human sentiments. According to Ives, music rose above any verbal analogies: "It was a language so transcendent, that its heights and depths, will be common to all mankind,"[13] as the technical means of composition were

---

[13] Ibid., p. 8.

expanded.

    In order to achieve this end, Ives was involved in the development of several new innovation techniques. He introduced quarter-tones in his music in the hope of "amplifying the spiritual consciousness." Ives felt that by increasing the technical possibilities of music, he could provide a greater freedom and even allow music to delve into the deeper region of the human sentiment. In so doing, music would continue as a transcendental language. "Because the soul is progressive, it never quite repeats itself, but in every act attempts the production of a new and fairer whole."[14]

Ives saw in music a fundamental duality of values: substance vs. manner. He believed that if the composer kept this duality in mind, the expression of the spiritual

---

[14] Ralph Waldo Emerson, "Art," Essays, (Boston: Houghton, Mifflin & Co., 1883), p. 327.

Dr. Paul A. Rodríguez

sentiments might be more clearly distinguished from the expression of the more immediate and superficial values of mankind. Ives considered substance the highest element of the duality, which was based upon "those kinds of unselfish human interests which we call knowledge and morality—knowledge, not in the sense of erudition, but as a kind of creation or creative truth."[15]

---

[15] Charles E. Ives, <u>Essays Before a</u>

An American Composer Charles E. Ives:
New England Transcendentalism

Ives regarded substance as the most important element in music and opposed the lower superficial values of form, quality, or manner. He defined substance as ". . . the body of a conviction which has its birth in the spiritual consciousness, whose youth is nourished in the moral consciousness, and whose maturity, as a result of all this growth, is then represented in

---

Sonata and Other Writings, (New York: Norton & Co., 1964), p. 75.

a mental image."[16]

Ives described manner as that which translates substance into expression. He seemed to imply, by manner, the technical and material aspects of music. Thus, beauty in its sensual or material sense was more closely related to manner.

Ives believed that beauty was, in its highest sense, a moral quality which

---

[16] Charles E. Ives, Essays Before a Sonata and Other Writings, (New York: Norton & Co., 1964), p. 75.

An American Composer Charles E. Ives:
New England Transcendentalism

would naturally be related to substance. However, Ives hesitated to accept beauty without some caution, since he often saw beauty connected with the sweet, habitual sounds of traditional 19th century music. Ives did not regard beauty as the highest value nor as the most fundamental element of musical substance. As he said of Emerson, he pursued truth, "not strength of outline or even beauty, except insofar as they might reveal themselves naturally in his explorations towards the infinite."[17] Emerson stated that a third class of men "live above the beauty of the symbol to the beauty of the thing signified"[18] and obtain a spiritual perception. Ives used the term "truth" to signify knowledge in the spiritual or moral sense. This spiritual truth, Ives

---

[17] Ibid., p. 21.
[18] Ralph Waldo Emerson, "Prudence," Essays, (Boston: Houghton, Mifflin & Co., 1883), p. 210.

An American Composer Charles E. Ives:
New England Transcendentalism

associated with the substance of music that was related to the moral character of the composer.

Ives believed that his theory of duality in music could help to explain the various phenomena of music and in particular modern music. He saw, in the overemphasis of nationalism in music, an evidence of manner gaining dominance over substance. The true spiritual qualities of mankind were produced in a universal mode, not a national character. For Ives, music must include more than a passing interest in the national and aspire toward the spiritual where all humanity has a common nature. The composer must associate a natural interest within his subject and feel the underlying spirit of its greatness. He must find cause to the extent of making it a part of his spiritual consciousness. That which he selects to represent the national, will be universal as his own high spiritual ideals coincide with those of his subject:

If his music can but catch that spirit by being a part with itself, it will come somewhere near his ideal—and it will be American too ... If local color, national color, any color, is a true pigment of the universal color, it is a divine quality, it is a part of substance in art—not of manner.[19]

In this way, local

---

[19] Charles E. Ives, <u>Essays Before a Sonata and Other Writings</u>, (New York: Norton & Co., 1964), p.18.

experiences of life could serve as shadows of higher qualities. As Ives said of Emerson, "He seems to use the great definite interests of humanity to express the greater, indefinite spiritual values – to fulfill what he can in his realms of revelation."[20] So likewise, the artist who attempts to create excellence in his work will do so intuitively when he finds an excellence in life.

In addition to substance

---

[20] Ibid., p. 29.

and manner, Ives saw another duality in music, that of truth and repose:

> God offers to every mind its choice between truth and repose. Take which you please, – you can never have both. Between these, as a pendulum, man oscillates.[21]

With repose, Ives associated the overemphasis of instrumental technique at the expense of idea. He felt that the technical elements of

---

[21] Ralph Waldo Emerson, "Intellect," Essays, (Boston: Houghton, Mifflin & Co., 1883), p. 318.

Dr. Paul A. Rodríguez

music, typical of the music of his day, were placing limitations upon music. Music, to Ives, was not sound but essentially idea. He saw the emphasis on music's physical effect as a sign, not only of a weakening of the music's quality, but of also a weakening of the composer's moral character. Repose was then seen as an overemphasis of manner as a value, leading to the massing together of instrumental effects.

An American Composer Charles E. Ives:
New England Transcendentalism

The instrument! —there is the perennial difficulty—there is music's limitations. Why must the scarecrow of the keyboard—the tyrant in terms of the mechanism—stare into every measure? Is it the composer's fault man has only ten fingers?[22]

It suggests that a composer becomes conscious of a style of his own. To quote one of Ives's more ironic statements, "Nothing can bring you peace but yourself.

---

[22] Charles E. Ives, <u>Essays Before a Sonata and Other Writings</u>, (New York: Norton & Co., 1964), p. 18.

Nothing can bring you peace but the triumph of principles."[23] Repose places an importance upon prize money, style, technique, etc. It fails to see the value of the common man.

For these reasons, Ives felt that an artistic activity was better if it became an involvement of life. If the musician were to look at his art, as the only thing worth considering, he would produce

---

[23] Ralph Waldo Emerson, "Self Reliance," Essays, (Boston: Houghton, Mifflin & Co., 1883), p. 87.

An American Composer Charles E. Ives:
New England Transcendentalism

the prejudices of the minority which favors only a given style.

In order to achieve an expression of the higher spiritual values, Ives believed that the musician must involve himself in ordinary life. In this matter, art might be a subconscious expression of the composer's innermost thoughts. These daily experiences must be supplemented by the composer's revelations of nature.

Dr. Paul A. Rodríguez

The true artist is willing to incorporate all into his art:

Let man then learn the revelation of all nature and all thought to his heart; this, namely; that the Highest dwells with him, that the sources of nature are in his own mind.[24]

Thus, it was from a spiritual point of view that Ives approached the intellectual and technical side of music. For Ives, the technical aspects

---

[24] Ralph Waldo Emerson, "The Over-Soul," <u>Essays</u>, (Boston: Houghton, Mifflin & Co., 1883), p. 276.

were necessary only in bringing out the spiritual truths. Ives considered composing as an outgrowth of an underlying spiritual or moral idea which found its expression in an appropriate set of sounds.

Hence, Ives's indebtedness to Emerson's transcendentalism decisively influenced his own subconscious interpretation of his music.

Dr. Paul A. Rodríguez

CHAPTER III

HENRY DAVID THOREAU'S CONTRIBUTIONS TO IVES'S AESTHETICS DEVELOPMENT

Ives's use of popular songs, hymns, and the like, is a distinguishing characteristic of his music. Ives once remarked:

My God! What has sound got
to do with music!
The waiter brings the only egg
he has, but the man
at breakfast sends it back
because it doesn't fit his
eggcup. Why can't music go
out in the same way it comes in
to a man, without thoraxes,
catguts, wire, wood and brass?[25]

Similarly, Ives's hero, Thoreau, centered his interest almost totally on the popular and sentimental ballads of the day. Indeed, Thoreau

---

[25] Charles E. Ives, <u>Essays Before a Sonata and Other Writings</u>, (New York: Norton & Co., 1964), p. 84.

expanded the definition of music as an art form. He construed sound and silence as forms of music, since silence may be considered musical, and sound an utterance of silence.

To quote Thoreau:

I rejoice that there are owls. Let them do the idiotic and manical hooting for men. It is a sound admirably suited to swamps and twilight woods which no day illustrates, suggesting a vast and undeveloped nature which men have not recognized.[26]

---

[26] Henry David Thoreau, Walden and

Dr. Paul A. Rodríguez

Ives viewed Thoreau as a personal friend. Whose freelance life style typified the Ivesian "rough way up the mountain" image and personified Transcendentalism's existential struggle with ultimate questions of being:

Is not beauty in music too often confused with something which lets the ears lie back in an easy-chair? Many sounds that we are used to do not

---

Other Writings of Henry David Thoreau, ed. By Brooks Atkinson, (New York: Random House Books, 1937), p. 114.

bother us, and for that reason are we not too easily inclined to call them beautiful?[27]

Ives saw nature as limitless; similarly, he viewed music as a limitless art form as well. If music has inferior qualities, those are produced by man's limitations:

> If it happens to feel like trying to fly where humans cannot fly, to sing what cannot be sung, to walk in a cave on all fours, or to tighten up its girth in blind hope and faith and try to scale

---

[27] Charles E. Ives, <u>Essays Before a Sonata and Other Writings</u>, (New York: W. W. Norton & Co., 1964), p. 125.

Dr. Paul A. Rodríguez

mountains that are not, who shall stop it?[28]

The listener of a work, "based to some extent on more than one or two rhythmic, melodic, or harmonic schemes," must play an active role in order to discover the inherent possibilities present. The listener may decide which levels of sound are in his mind. In addition, he may fluctuate his concentration between the

---

[28] Charles E. Ives, <u>Essays Before a Sonata and Other Writings</u>, (New York: W. W. Norton & Co., 1964), p. 131.

An American Composer Charles E. Ives:
New England Transcendentalism

various levels of sound, or he may recall the distant sound of a familiar melody which acquires a new significant meaning in his mind. Therefore, the importance of music does not even lie exclusively in the musical sounds themselves. Instead, the significance of music lies in its capacity to become a part of the inner consciousness of man, rather than limiting his dreams and thoughts.

    Since Ives disliked the

Dr. Paul A. Rodríguez

traditional limitations which academic concepts of harmony, rhythm, form, etc. placed upon music, he rejected the notion of renationalizing in music. In Ives's view, musical unity was the expression of music as apprehended by human intuition. When this unifying element is understood by the intuition, it is immediately appreciated and separated from the formal or technical details which are appraised by the intellect. Ives believed that a work does not equally reveal its spiritual unity. He believed that an over-exaggeration of formal techniques would produce an indubitable dullness. As Ives saw it, the composer who relies upon this kind of unity could lose his substance:

> The intensity today with which techniques and media are organized and used tends to throw the mind away from a "common sense" and towards manner, and thus to resultant weak and mental states.[29]

---

[29] Ibid.), p. 91.

Dr. Paul A. Rodríguez

Thoreau believed that nature contains all the realities of the universe. The poet and artist utilize nature as a design for their art. To quote Thoreau:

God himself culminates in the present moment, and will never be more divine in the lapse of all the ages. And we are enabled to apprehend at all what is sublime and noble only by the perpetual instilling and drenching of the reality that surrounds us. Let us spend one day as deliberately as Nature, and not be thrown off the track by every nutshell and mosquito's wing that falls on

An American Composer Charles E. Ives:
New England Transcendentalism

the rails.[30]

Ives desired to protect against the confusion which might result when intellectual designs were perceived as intuitive expressions. He believed that these two artistic elements were to be considered separately in order to apprehend their individual worth. As Ives said of Thoreau:

---

[30] Henry David Thoreau, Walden and Other Writings of Henry David Thoreau, ed. By Brooks Atkinson, (New York: Random House Books, 1937), p. 87.

Dr. Paul A. Rodríguez

Thoreau's susceptibility to natural sounds was probably greater than that of many practical musicians. Thoreau seems able to weave . . . some perfectly transcendental symphonies. It was the soul of Nature, not natural history that Thoreau was after. He seems rather to let Nature put him under her microscope than to hold her under his.[31] For Thoreau, Nature

represented a constant source

of life:

I went to the woods because I wished to live deliberately, to front only the essential facts of

---

[31] Charles E. Ives, <u>Essays Before a Sonata and Other Writings</u>, (New York: W. W. Norton & Co., 1964), pp. 53-54.

life, and see that I could not learn what it had to teach, and not, when I came to die, discover that I had not lived. I did not wish to live what was not life, living is so dear; nor did I wish to practice resignation unless it was quite necessary. I wanted to live deep and suck out all the marrow of life.[32]

Ives considered that unity in music, which was created through rational exposition, was "easy unity."

---

[32] Henry David Thoreau, Walden and Other Writings of Henry David Thoreau, (New York: Random House Books, 1937), p. 81.

Dr. Paul A. Rodríguez

He associated such formal techniques with the sonata-allegro form:

A first theme, a development, a second in a related key and its development, the free fantasia, the recapitulation, and so on, and over again. Mr. Richter or Mr. Parker may tell us that this is natural, for it is based on the classic-song form.[33]

Ives felt that the sonata-allegro form had been "stretched out into deformity." This deformity was, in part, the

---

[33] Charles E. Ives, <u>Essays Before a Sonata and Other Writings</u>, (New York: W. W. Norton & Co., 1964), p. 99.

result of an over-reliance upon repetition. Repetition, for Ives, reveals a state of permanence and nature is ever changing and in a constant state of flux:

> Nature loves analogy and hates repetition. Botany reveals evolution, not permanence. Initial coherence today may be dullness tomorrow, probably because formal or outward unity depends so much on repetition.[34]

As Thoreau said of Nature and life:

---

[34] Charles E. Ives, Essays Before a Sonata and Other Writings, (New York: W. W. Norton & Co., 1964), p. 22-23.

Dr. Paul A. Rodríguez

But man's capacities have never been measured; nor are we to judge of what he can do by any precedents, so little has been tried. . . . Nature and human life are as various as our several constitutions. Who shall say what prospect life offers to another?[35]

Ives saw a great deal of repetition in Beethoven's music. Yet, he fully understood that Beethoven handled classical forms with freedom and genius. To quote

---

[35] Henry David Thoreau, "Economy" <u>The Writings of Henry David Thoreau.</u> (New York: Walden Edition, 1906), p. 11.

An American Composer Charles E. Ives:
New England Transcendentalism

Ives:

Beethoven had to churn, to some extent, to make his message carry. He had to pull the ear, hard and in the same place and several times, for the 1790 ear was tougher than the 1890 one.[36]

He felt that by the end of the 19th century, the traditional standardized formal procedures, prevented music from technically progressing and placed unnecessary limitations upon it. Ives's

---

[36] Charles E. Ives, Essays Before a Sonata and Other Writings, (New York: W. W. Norton & Co., 1964), p. 99.

important concept about musical unity would allow the composer perfect freedom and fully realize the individuality of his musical elements:

... everyone should be as free as possible to encourage everyone, including himself, to work and to be willing to work where this interest directs, 'to stand and be willing to stand unprotected from all the showers of the absolute which may beat upon him, to use or learn to use, or at least be unafraid of trying to use, whatever he can of any and all lessons of the infinite which humanity has received and thrown to him, that Nature has

An American Composer Charles E. Ives:
New England Transcendentalism

exposed and sacrificed for him, that life and death have translated for him, until the products of his labor shall beat around and through his ordinary work – shall strengthen, widen, and deepen all his senses, aspirations, or whatever the innate power and impulses may be called, which God has given man.[37]

Such freedom would bring

every man to the point where

he is an artist and writes his

own music, music as free as the

composer who created it:

. . . until the day will come

---

[37] Ibid., p. 128.

Dr. Paul A. Rodríguez

when every man while digging his potatoes will breathe his own epics, his own symphonies (operas, if he like it); and as he sits of an evening in his backyard and shirt sleeves smoking his pipe and watching his brave children in their fun of building their themes for their sonatas of their life, he will look up over the mountains and see his visions in their reality, will hear the transcendental strains of the day's symphony resounding in their many choirs, and in all their perfection, through the west wind and tree tops![38]

---

[38] Charles E. Ives, Essays Before a Sonata and Other Writings, (New York: W. W. Norton & Co., 1964), pp. 128-219.

An American Composer Charles E. Ives:
New England Transcendentalism

Thoreau expressed comparable sentiments about populist art:

I learned this, at least, by my experiment; that if one advances confidently in the direction of his dreams and endeavors to live the life which he has imagined, he will meet with success unexpected in common hours. He will pass an invisible boundary; new, universal, and more liberal laws will begin to establish themselves around and within him.[39]

In Thoreau's mind,

---

[39] Henry David Thoreau, "Conclusion", The Writings of Henry David Thoreau. (New York: Walden Edition, 1906), p. 356.

society provided too many material boundaries which were ends into themselves:

> It lives too fast. Men think that it is essential that the Nation have commerce, and export ice, and talk through a telegraph, and ride thirty miles an hour, without a doubt, whether they do or not; but whether we should live like baboons or like men, is a little uncertain.[40]

Hence, Ives rejected an overemphasis of the traditional

---

[40] Henry David Thoreau, <u>Walden and Other Writings of Henry David Thoreau</u>, ed. By Brooks Atkinson, (New York: Random House Books, 1937), p. 83.

An American Composer Charles E. Ives:
New England Transcendentalism

in music because it placed, in his opinion, unnatural limits upon the future development of music. However, he did not reject all traditional concepts of music because that would have contradicted his view concerning the value of past developments and discoveries of mankind. Indeed, he believed that past developments and discoveries were an important element of the intuition. In addition, Ives expected that the technical

Dr. Paul A. Rodríguez

aspects of music could be placed in their proper perspective, so as not to overshadow the more important spiritual and moral values of music. The healthiest attitude toward music should be directed towards the spiritual, rather than the technical, directed him toward a reverence for the ideals and hopes of the past:

If you have built castles in the aid, your work need not be lost; that is where they should be. Now put the foundations under them. Let him step to

An American Composer Charles E. Ives:
New England Transcendentalism

the music which he hears, however measured or far away. It is not important that he should mature as soon as an apple tree or an oak.[41]

Ives wanted to avoid logical rationalizing in music which would result from the overuse of musical techniques. Simultaneously, he wanted to retain certain qualities of traditional music he felt were valuable. He does not specify the traditional elements, which

[41] Henry David Thoreau, The Writings of Henry David Thoreau, (New York: Walden Edition, 1906), pp. 356-359.

Dr. Paul A. Rodríguez

he opined worthy of retention in music. Equivocally, he does not elicit the mean whereby the traditional modes of thematic and formal construction, based upon repetition, might be avoided, nor to what extent he desires to avoid such developmental procedures. Several of his early piano works rely heavily on traditional methods of composition, such as <u>Varied Air and Variations</u>, <u>Invention</u>, <u>March in G and D</u> "<u>Here's to</u>

Good Old Yale." Other works show an obvious break with previous procedures of the past; for example, The Anti-Abolitionist Riots and The Celestial Railroad. His later works developed the stylistic features that came to be associated with his compositions. These methods included polytonality, polymetricality, whole-tone scales, complex rhythmic groups and frequent quotation of patriotic tunes, hymn melodies, "familiar" rhythmic patterns and harmonic progressions.

Insofar as Ives was indebted to Thoreau in formulating his concept of unity in music, the stylistic features of his compositions demonstrate that he was able to realize his personal vision, sincerity, and freedom within a framework of spiritual unity.

Unlike his contemporary, Ralph Waldo Emerson, Thoreau was a

An American Composer Charles E. Ives:
New England Transcendentalism

revolutionary who created an articulate literature of revolt. Contrary to Emerson, Thoreau disassociated himself from society and established himself as a powerful social critic. While the romanticism of that time preached Nature's power and beauty, and while Emerson meditated upon and interpreted Nature to suit himself, Thoreau lived and thought of himself as a subject of Nature.

      Thoreau's practical

Dr. Paul A. Rodríguez

skills and thorough acquaintance with the Concord countryside allowed him to earn his living as a surveyor for the remainder of his life. Hence, Thoreau separated his avocation from his occupation. Similarly, Ives's life style reflected Thoreau's in that he earned a living from the life insurance business and not from his music.

    Thoreau's knowledge of natural history, and his deep desire for communion with nature, differentiated him from the rest of Emerson's circle. Like Emerson, Thoreau held little belief in collective protests against the existing social order. For him, Thoreau, Nature was more fundamental than relationships with other men.

    Like Thoreau, Ives struggled with society's rejection of his art, but he persevered with the hope that someday his music would surpass its outward sounding

Dr. Paul A. Rodríguez

appearance and receive its rightful appreciation. He did not expect an audience to grasp the musical logic of his works because, at times, an author or composer may, of necessity, appear formless to his audience. The philosophical beliefs of the New England Transcendentalists offered Ives the means to create any sounds which were true to his own sense of reason and a justification to compose with

An American Composer Charles E. Ives: New England Transcendentalism

whatever logic he decided upon.

Ives's knowledge of Emerson's aesthetics was part of his defense against critical, invective, and uninteresting musical styles. Ives was able to assimilate the Transcendental belief of individual creative realities. Like Emerson, he recognized the composer's genuine ability to create artistic substance rather than superficial manner.

Ives was affected by

Emerson's continual struggle for artistic, social, and moral excellence. Ives spoke about Emerson's ability to leave impressions upon those who listened to him lecture:

> It mattered little what party or what platform or what law of commerce governed men. Was man governing himself? Social error and virtue were but relative. This habit of not being hindered by using, but still going beyond, the great truths of life gave force to his influence over the materialists.[42]

---

[42] Charles E. Ives, <u>Essays Before a Sonata and Other Writings</u>, (New York: W. W. Norton & Co., 1964), p. 27.

Therefore, Emerson represented a type of universal spirituality to Ives; while Thoreau's communion with Nature strengthened his will for individuality.

Dr. Paul A. Rodríguez

CHAPTER IV

CONCLUSION

This thesis of Charles Ives's piano works hasdemonstrated how the composer transformed the New England Transcendentalism into a personal musical expression. Through the influence of the New

Dr. Paul A. Rodríguez

England Transcendentalists, Ives developed many progressive concepts about musical compositions. In particular, no rejected the academic idea that musical compositions should be viewed as merely formalistic works and that musical notion only expressed the intention of the composer. Indeed Ives's aesthetics envisioned a new artistic union of the composer, performer and listener - a creative synthesis

An American Composer Charles E. Ives:
New England Transcendentalism

that was substantiated by the
selected piano work.
Insofar as Ives exemplified
a fatherly affection toward his
compositions, shaping them
and bestowing upon them
his continuing attention as
time passed,his attitude
toward the performers
of his music was likewise
apprehensive.
By means of the Essays and
marginalia comments, Ives has
sought to instruct the player
or scholar how to think about

Dr. Paul A. Rodríguez

each composition, when to use various versions, how to finger the work, interpret it, change it, make it easier and ultimately advises to do whatever seems natural. The tremendous magnitude of these communications to the performer may be overwhelming and sometimes confusing, "but ultimately, the overall impression is that the performer is expected to contribute to the evolving

An American Composer Charles E. Ives:
New England Transcendentalism

character of each work, and that Ives was more concerned that the music prevail than the "right" notes he played. Ives developed a musical syntax which illustrated the application of his aesthetic and shoved the extent of which New England Transcendentalism influenced that aesthetic. The manner in which the composer amalgamated these elements into a personal

expression of the
Transcendental ethic was
carefully illustrated. As an
outgrowth of his
Transcendental beliefs and his
demand for "substance"
in music, Ives realised the
importance of allowing the
performer to share in the
creative process of the
composition* to have a choice
of moods, tempo and even
notes, to the extent of calling in
a second player. Insofar as
Ives was sincere in his

An American Composer Charles E. Ives:
New England Transcendentalism

many requests for a broader, freer treatment of the compositions, the player then has a responsibility to come to a point of greater appreciation and fulfillment of these requests.
The New England Transcendentalist believed that the common, the familiar and the natural were links to a higher spiritual world. Ultimately, Ives's transcendental philosophy would be his reconciliation

Dr. Paul A. Rodríguez

of a physical world with a
spiritual reality-
Ives created a human
consciousness in his music by
inserting tunes which had a
prior association in the mind
of the listener an certain
mechanical controls to
represent the movement of con
sciousness in music.
For example, his
"human fate motive", in <u>The
Anti-Abolitlonist Riots,</u>
represented the universality
of the common man.

An American Composer Charles E. Ives:
New England Transcendentalism

Ives believed that the desire to create must have a share in ordinary life in order to he an expression of the higher spiritual values.
Music must be a part of the subconscious expression of the composer. Thus, Ives insertion of familiar tunes in <u>Waltz—Rondo</u> expresses his impressions and sentiments of Arlington cemetery, and his rapid passages in <u>Celestial Railroad</u> represent a train ride.

Dr. Paul A. Rodríguez

Ives's compositional style was an outgrowth of his spiritual or moral ideas which found its expression in an appropriate group of sounds. Therefore, in Ives's view, experimentation with various sonorities and rhythmic groupings was to bring the inner content of his music to a deeper realisation. For example, experiments with polytonalities in the <u>Three-Page Sonata</u> and

An American Composer Charles E. Ives:
New England Transcendentalism

<u>Some Southpaw Pitching</u>,
bore for Ives a special
significance.

Along with borrowed tunes,
Ives choice of subject
matter exemplifies his preoccu
pation with conditions and
manners existing in America.
Ives agreed with Emerson's
dictum not to seek outside the
self, and composed music
which depicted life in America,
as seen in the compositions
<u>Some Southpaw Pitching</u>,

Dr. Paul A. Rodríguez

<u>March in G and D "Here's to Good Old Yale"</u> amd <u>The Anti-Abolitionist Riots</u>.

      In conclusion, Ives's compositional style is truly indebted to the belief's of the New England Transcendentalists. The piano compositions chosen for this book amplify the necessity to continue to investigate and appreiate the compositional style of the American compser, Charles E. Ives.

REFERENCES

Austin, William F. (1966). *Music in the twentieth century: Debussy through Stravinsky.* New York, NY: W. W. Norton.

Bellamann, Henry. (1933). Charles Ives: The man and his music. *Musical Quarterly 19*: 45-58.

Blum, William Anson. (1971). A study of the transcendental aesthetics theories of John S. Dwight and Charles E. Ives and the relationship of these theories of their respective work as music critics and composer. Respective work as music critics and composer." (Ph.D. Dissertation, University of Illinois).

Carter, Elliott. (1944). Ives today: His vision and challenger. *Modern Music,21*: 199-202.

Carter, Elliott. (1955). The rhythmic basis of American music. *Score 12*: 29-31.

Cazden, Norman. (1955). Realism in abstract music. *Music and Letters, 36*: 17.

Clark, Sondra Rae. (1972). *The evolving Concord Sonata: A study of choices and variants in the music of Charles Ives."* (Ph.D. Dissertation, Stanford University).

Clark, Sondra Rae. (1974). The element of choice in Ives's Concord Sonata. *Musical Quarterly, 10*: 167-186.

Clarke, Henry Leland. (1964). Essays before a sonata: A review. *Musical Quarterly, 50*: 101-103.

Cohn, Arthur. (1969). Alan Mandel plays all 27 of the piano works of Ives." *American Record Guide, 35*: 548-549.

Copland, Aaron.(1961). A business man who wrote music on Sunday. *Music and Musicians, 9*: 18.

Cowell, Henry Ed. (1933). *American composers on American music: A symposium.* Stanford, CA: Stanford University Press.

Cowell, Henry Ed. (1932). Charles Ives. *Modern Music, 10*: 24-32.

Cowell, Henry Ed. (1949). Chronological relationship of only three works for piano by Charles Ives. *Musical Quarterly, 35*: 459-462.

Cowell, Henry, & Cowell, Sidney. (1955). *Charles Ives and his Music*. New York, NY: Oxford University Press.

Cyr, Gordon. (1971, fall/winter). Intervallic structural elements in Ives's Fourth Symphony. *Perspectives of New Music, 10*: 291-303.

Davidson, Audrey. (1970). Transcendental unity in the works of Charles Ives. *American Quarterly, 22*: 35-44.

Emerson, Ralph Waldo. (1833). *Essays. Vols I-XIV*. Boston, MA: Houghton, Mifflin & Co..

Emerson, Ralph Waldo. (1903-1904). *The complete works of Ralph Waldo Emerson*. New York, NY: Centenary Edition.

Frothingham, Octavious Books. (1903). *Transcendentalism in New England*. Boston, MA: American Unitarian Association.

Goddard, Harold C. (1960). *Studies in New England Transcendentalism*. New York, NY: Columbia University Press.

Harris, Neil. (1966). *The artist in American society*. New York, NY: George Braziller.

Harrison, Lou. (1946). On Quotation. *Modern Music, 23*: 166-169.

Henderson, Clayton. (1974). Ives's use of quotation. *Music Educators Journal, 61*: 24-28.

Henderson, Clayton. (1969). *Quotation as a style element in the music of Charles Ives*. (Ph.D. Dissertation, Washington University).

Hitchcock, Wile H. (1969). *Music in the United States: A historical introduction.* New Jersey: Prentice Hall, Inc.

Hitchcock, Wile H. (1977). *Ives.* New York, NY: Oxford University Press.

Hotchfield, George, Ed. Selected Writings of the American Transcendentalists. New York: The New American Library, 1966.

Ives, Charles E. (1964). *Essays before a sonata and other writings.* Ed. By Howard Boatwright. New York: Norton & Co., 1964.

Ives, Charles E. (1972). *Charles E. Ives: Memos*. Ed. By John Kirkpatrick. New York. NY: W.W. Norton & Co.

Ives, Charles E. (1933). Music and its Future. Ed. By Henry Cowell, *American Composers on American Music*. Stanford, CA: Stanford University Press.

Ives, Charles E. *The Complete Works for Piano*. Program Notes by Alan Mandel. Desto Records, DST 6458-6461.

Ives, Charles E. *The short piano pieces of Charles Ives*. James Sykes, piano. Folkways Records, FM 3348.

Josephson, Nors S. (1978). Charles Ives: Intervallische Permutationen im Spatwerk. *Zeitschrift für Musiktheorie 9*: 27-33.

Josephson, Nors S. (1974). Zur formalin Struktur einiger spatter Orchesterkwerke von Charles Ives (1874-1954. *Die Musiforschung 27 #1*: 57-64.

Joyce, Sister Mary Ann, C.S.J. (1970). *The "Three Page-Sonata" of Charles Ives: An analysis and a corrected version."* (Ph.D. Dissertation, Washington University, 1970).

Kirkpatrick, John. (1960). *A Temporary Mimeographed Catalogue of Music Manuscripts and Related*

Dr. Paul A. Rodríguez

Materials of Charles E. Ives, 1874-1954. Unpublished catalogue. New Haven: Demander Book Bindery, Inc.

Kirkpatrick, John. (1949). The Anti-Abolitionist Riots in the 1950's for Piano Solo. *Music Library Association Notes* 6: 486-487.

Kirkpatrick, John. (1963). What music meant to Charles Ives. *Cornell University Music Review,* 6: 13-18.

Koster, Donald Nelson. (1975). *Transcendentalism in America.* Boston, MA: Twayne Publishers.

Lang, Paul Henry. (1946). Charles Ives, Hearing Things. *Saturday Review of Literature, 29*: 43.

Leighton, Walter L. (1908). *French philosophers and New England Transcendentalism.* Charlottesville, VA: University of Virginia Press.

Lerma, Dominique-Rene de. (1970). *Charles Edward Ives, 1874-1954, Bibliography of his music.* Kent, OH: Kent State University Press.

Marshall, Dennis. (1968). Charles Ives's quotations: Manner or substance. *Perspectives of New Music* 6: 45-56.

Miller, Perry, ed. (1957). *The American Transcendentalists: Their prose and poetry.* New York: Doubleday & Co., Inc.

Miller, Perry, ed. (1967). *The Transcendentalists: An anthology.* Cambridge, MA: Harvard University Press.

Perlis, Vivian. (1974). *Charles Ives remembered.* New Haven, CT: Yale University Press.

Perry, Rosalie Sandra. (1974) *Charles Ives and the American mind.* Kent, OH: Kent State University Press.

Perry, Rosalie Sandra. (1971). *Charles Ives and American culture.* (Ph.D. Dissertation, University of Texas at Austin).

Reis, Claire. (1932). *American composers.* New York: International Society for Contemporary Music

Ringer, Alexander L. (1974). Musical taste and the industrial syndrome: A sociological problem in historical analysis. *International Review of the Aesthetics and Sociology of Music 5*: 150-152.

Reti, Rudolph. (1958). *Tonality, atonality, pantonality: A study of some trends in twentieth-century music.* New York: MacMillan & Co.

Rider, Daniel E. (1964). *The musical thought and activities of the New England Transcendentalists*. (Ph.D. Dissertation, University of Minnesota).

Reinhart, John McLain. (1970). *Ives's compositional idioms: An investigation of selected short compositions as microcosmos of his musical language.* (Ph.D. Dissertation, Ohio State University).

Rosenfield, Paul. (1932) Charles E. Ives. *The New Republic* 71: 262-264.

Rossi, Nick, & Coats, Robert A. (1969). *Music of our time*. Boston, MA: Crescendo Publishing Co.

Rossiter, Frank R. (1975). *Charles Ives and his America*. New York: Liveright.

Sachs, Curt. (1953). *Rhythm and tempo*. New York, NY: W. W. Norton & Co.

Salzman, Eric. (1968). Charles Ives, American. *Commentary 46*: 37-43.

Salzman, Eric. (1968). The piano music of Charles Ives." *High Fidelity Review:* 72-73.

Schermer, Richard. (1980). *The aesthetics of Charles Ives in relation to "His String Quartet No. 2."* (Master of Arts Thesis, California State University, Fullerton).

Schrade, Leo. (1955). Charles E. Ives: 1874-1954. *Yale Review, 44*: 435-445.

Starr, Lawrence. (1977, May). Charles Ives: The next hundred years towards a method of analyzing the music. *The Music Review 38.*

Stuckenschmidt, H. H. (1972). *Twentieth-Century music.* Translated by Richard Deveson. New York, NY: McGraw-Hill Book Co.

Thomason, Virgil. (1971). *Twentieth-Century composers: American music since 1910.* New York, NY: Holt, Rinehart & Winston.

Thoreau, Henry David. (1966). *Walden and civil disobedience.* Ed. By Owen Thomas. New York, NY: W. W. Norton & Co., 1966.

Thoreau, Henry David. (1906). *The writings of Henry David Thoreau.* Walden Edition. Boston, MA: Houghton Mifflin Co.

Wallach, Lawrence David.(1974). *The New England Education of Charles Ives.* (Ph.D. Dissertation, Columbia University).

Ward, Charles Wilson. (1974). *Charles Ives: The Relationship Between Aesthetic Theories and Compositional Processes.* (Ph.D. Dissertation, University of Texas at Austin).

Ward, Charles Wilson. (1969). *The use of hymn tunes as an expression of substance and manner in the music of Charles E. Ives, 1874-1954.* (Master's Thesis, University of Texas at Austin).

Warren, Richard, Jr. (1972). *Charles E. Ives discography.* New Haven, CT: Yale University Library.

Wiley, Joan M. (1981). *A comparative analysis of Charles E. Ives' "First Sonata" and "Sonata No. 2."* (Master of Arts Thesis, California State University, Fullerton).

Wittlich, Gary E., ed. (1975). *Aspects of Twentieth-Century music.*

An American Composer Charles E. Ives:
New England Transcendentalism

Englewood Cliffs, NJ: Prentice-Hall, Inc.

Wooldridge, David. (1974). *From the steeples and mountains.* New York: Aldred A. Knopf, Inc.

Wooldridge, David. (1967). *Twentieth-Century music: Its evolution from the end of the harmonic era into the present of sound.* New York: Pantheon Books, 1967.

Yates, Peter. (1950). Charles Ives. *Art and Architecture* 67.

Dr. Paul A. Rodríguez

DISCOGRAPHY

Ives, Charles E. *Music of Ives*. Berstein; Schuller; Biggs; Smith Singers; Stokowski; Boatwright; Ives, etc., 100th Anniversary, 4-Columbia.

Ives, Charles E. *Piano Music* (Complete) Deutach, pianist. 4-VOX SVBX5482

Ives, Charles E. *Piano Music* (Complete) Mandel, pianist. 4-Desto 6458/61.Ives, Charles E. *Piano Music in America*. Vol. 2, (1900-1945) Shields, pianist. 3-VOX SVNX53

ABOUT THE AUTHOR

Dr. Rodríguez is an educational leader focused on supporting local, state and national initiatives and programs. Dr. Rodriguez is a member of various educational organizations, including, the California League of High Schools and Association of California Administrators, as well as a California Awards for Performance Excellence California state senior examiner, Distinguished Schools, Schools to Watch and Gold Ribbon Awards.
Dr. Rodríguez has been in the educational profession for over thirty-six years, having served as an elementary teacher, high school guidance counselor, and

Dr. Paul A. Rodríguez

high school principal, in addition to, lecturer/presenter for state, national and higher education.
Contact and visit Dr. Paul A. Rodriguez at

par913@me.com

http://www.par913edu.com

http://www.californiacommoncorestandards.com

www.ingramcontent.com/pod-product-compliance
Lightning Source LLC
Chambersburg PA
CBHW070517100426
42743CB00010B/1847